Original title:
A Purposeful Journey in Pajamas

Copyright © 2025 Creative Arts Management OÜ
All rights reserved.

Author: Vivienne Beaumont
ISBN HARDBACK: 978-1-80566-111-5
ISBN PAPERBACK: 978-1-80566-406-2

The Unraveled Journey

Slippers squeak on the wooden floor,
Lost in dreams, who could ask for more?
A coffee spill, a cereal fight,
All dressed up, but it's still night.

Chasing toys with a languid grace,
In fluffy pants, I pick up the pace.
The cats all stare as I zoom around,
In this soft quest, silliness is found.

Mysterious Journeys in Soft Drapes

Under covers, a world unfolds,
With mysteries that are bright and bold.
A treasure map made of breakfast crumbs,
To find the socks, hear the laundry drums.

I crawl through cushions, a secret spy,
In pajama land, I can't let this fly!
With a cape of flannel, I'm ready to race,
Unleashing chaos, I rule this place.

Soles of Serenity

With each step on the carpeted plane,
I wander places both silly and plain.
In mismatched socks, I run this town,
A hero in pajamas, never a frown.

The fridge is a castle, the couch is a throne,
Features of comfort in every zone.
Guarded by snacks and endless delight,
I'm on a quest and it feels just right.

The Veil of Cozy Escapades

In the realm of warmth, where laughter flies,
Adventure awaits with pajama ties.
Pillow fights break the morning's calm,
With chuckles that wrap like a cozy balm.

With a donut hat and a blanket cape,
I slide on the floor, oh, what an escape!
Every corner hides a new playful jest,
In the land of pajamas, I'm truly blessed.

Pajama Dreams at Dawn

In fuzzy pants, I start my day,
Chasing dreams that drift away.
A cereal bath, I take a leap,
Wearing slippers, cozy and cheap.

Socks that clash, a wild display,
My fashion sense? Let's just say,
With every step, a giggle flows,
As I prance by, everyone knows.

Soft Canvas of Exploration

Exploring my house, a thrilling quest,
In my jammies, I feel so blessed.
Couch cushions turned to mountains high,
I'm an adventurer, soaring the sky.

In the fridge, I find a snack,
While wearing my panda-patterned slack.
Every room's a land unknown,
On this soft canvas, I've brightly grown.

Starlit Routes in Flannel

Under the stars in my flannel best,
I roam the yard, a pajama fest.
Fireflies twinkle, lighting the way,
In my nighttime garb, I dance and play.

A raccoon stares, I grin and wave,
In this fearless outfit, I'm oh so brave.
Around the trees, I make my mark,
Pajama-clad, I rule the dark.

The Clad Traveler's Quest

A quest for snacks, my heart's delight,
In my jammy gear, I take to flight.
TV remotes are treasure rare,
I search for chips hiding somewhere.

On this journey, I am the king,
In fluffy socks, I laugh and sing.
With a pillow fort as my throne,
I conquer the couch, never alone.

Bedtime Paths and Morning Dreams

In fluffy socks, I take my stroll,
Midnight snacks my ultimate goal.
Blanket fort, my castle grand,
With teddy bears, I make my stand.

Worn-out slippers squeak loud and clear,
Chasing shadows, nothing to fear.
Pajamas bright, a fashion claim,
My cozy style, the night-time game.

The Pajama Pilgrim's Way

With each step in my vibrant threads,
I wander past the sleepy heads.
Soft prints dance like stars above,
In this land, there's only love.

A pillow fight, the perfect scheme,
I gather strength from every dream.
Adventurous quests under the moon,
I conquer foes with a rubber spoon.

Soft Fabric, Bold Dreams

Cotton clouds above my feet,
Waking up near breakfast treat.
Over the hill, pajamas fly,
Cereal surprises make me sigh.

With a sleep mask as my shield,
I roam gardens, conquering fields.
Each groggy step is full of glee,
In mismatched socks, I'm wild and free.

Whimsical Wanders in Woven Comfort

In my jammies, I go roam,
Each corner here feels just like home.
Dancing lights, they twinkle bright,
As I explore the fridge at night.

Waves of sheets are calling me,
To dream of lands, both brave and free.
I'll wear my crown of fluffy warm,
A royal giggle, a bedtime charm.

Pajama Chronicles

In my jammies, I stride with ease,
Slippers squeaking, I aim to please.
Waving at neighbors, coffee in hand,
Who knew this outfit was so grand?

Finding treasures near the fridge,
Forgotten snacks, a guilty smidge.
Beneath the stars, I take my stand,
Pajama-clad, a brave night planned.

Each step a giggle, each turn a cheer,
In these cozy threads, I shed all fear.
I'm the ruler of this comfy realm,
In fluffy pants, I overwhelm.

With dogs in tow, we march along,
Our pajamas echo with a silly song.
Who needs a map or a fancy guide?
Adventure awaits with fluff as our pride.

Cloth-Draped Paths

Socks mismatched, what a sight,
Stumbling forward, oh what a fright!
On this journey from couch to bed,
In my fabric fortress, dreams are fed.

The cat, my co-pilot, sprawled wide,
Unbothered by the world outside.
Snack crumbs as our guiding stars,
Navigating through home's bizarre.

Under the blanket, whispers ignite,
Each silly plan makes the mood just right.
From the hallway's maze to the bathroom stall,
Laughing so hard, we might just fall.

Every corner holds a surprise,
With pajama comfort, joy never dies.
Here's to adventures in patterned attire,
Our escapades fueled by laughter's fire.

The Gentle Explorer's Expedition

With my trusty slippers, I set forth,
Into the wilds of my kitchen's north.
Bacon frying, coffee brewing,
With a belt of pajamas, I'm ready for pursuing.

A couch cushion mountain, I ascend,
Pillowed peaks that round the bend.
Daring to leap from chair to chair,
In this jungle, I'm beyond compare.

The pantry's depths hide treasures galore,
Leftover pizza, I explore.
Each bite a thrill, I laugh and grin,
In these cozy threads, let the fun begin!

Through laughter and crumbs, my quest unfolds,
In my soft attire, the bravest holds.
With friends by my side, the journey's a blast,
Pajama explorer, our joy unsurpassed.

Stitched Stories Under the Stars

Twinkling lights above my head,
Wrapped in comfort, thoughts widely spread.
Whispers of dreams flowing around,
In this soft cocoon, adventure is found.

The moon a witness to our late-night chat,
In pajamas, together, just me and my cat.
Laughter erupts—a truth or a myth,
Every fabric woven tells a tale or a skit.

We giggle at the stories the night unfolds,
In these dream-chasers, we find pure gold.
Our minds wander, exploring what's near,
Under flannel skies, there's nothing to fear.

So here we snuggle, our spirits high,
In stitched tales, together we fly.
With every outlandish thought we've shared,
In pajamas, oh, what joy is declared!

Whispers of the Night Attire

In fluffy socks and cozy pants,
I tiptoe softly, take my stance.
The fridge is calling, oh so near,
A midnight feast, my secret cheer.

Ghosts of snacks haunt every shelf,
I raid them all, I've lost myself.
With crumbs and giggles, I parade,
A pajama bandit unafraid.

The cat looks on, a judging glare,
While I indulge without a care.
Each bite is music, sweet delight,
In jammies, the world feels just right.

So here I am, in nighttime gear,
Laughing softly, sipping beer.
For in this realm of soft delight,
Adventure waits in every bite.

Silk and Serenity

In silky sheets, I find my way,
Embracing dreams that loves convey.
A puddle of giggles on the floor,
As I trip on pillows, seeking more.

A cup of cocoa, warmth in hand,
I plan my escape to a chocolate land.
With every sip, my dreams expand,
Dancing through dreams, oh so unplanned.

Each little snore of bear-like delight,
Echoes of laughter ftom the night.
In these soft threads, anxieties fade,
Midnight escapades, unafraid.

With every twist of pajama cloth,
I conquer kingdoms, never sloth.
For in this silk, my spirit flies,
A whimsical journey, under starlit skies.

Pathway of the Sleepy Explorer

With mismatched socks, I roam so free,
Exploring realms of mystery.
My trusty teddy leads the way,
Through wild adventures, come what may.

A few more steps, oh what's that sound?
The fridge? It calls! Treasure found!
In jammies, I embark on quests,
Where midnight snacks are my best guests.

I'm sneaking treats, a sneaky spy,
As moonlight dances in the sky.
Each journey's a giggle, a funny feat,
In soft attire, what a tasty treat!

As mornings come, dreams may fade,
But memories of snacks will not be swayed.
For every stumble, each gummy bear,
In PJs, I've conquered everywhere.

Untamed Journeys in Jammies

The backyard calls, a vast terrain,
In flannel dreams, I'll stake my claim.
With a blanket cape, an aviator's flair,
I zoom through night with pajama wear.

A brave explorer on a quest,
In damp grass, I do my best.
With worms as friends, I share my tales,
Of teddy bears and wind-filled sails.

The moonlight guides my pajama flight,
As shadows dance, what a sight!
In each curious nook, fun unfolds,
With whispers of magic, brave and bold.

So here's to journeys, both wild and grand,
With every misstep, life's sweet blend.
In jammies, we laugh, we play the role,
Of untamed spirits with a cozy goal.

Pajama Horizons and Cozy Seas

In fluffy clouds we sail away,
Our pajamas billow, come what may.
With a cup of cocoa in hand,
We tour the land, oh isn't it grand!

From bed to couch, we wander wide,
In soft attire, it's quite the ride.
Pajama parties turn to quests,
In sleepy garb, we are the best!

The dog joins in, a sight to see,
In matching pjs, oh, what glee!
Unruly hair, misfit styles,
We conquer worlds with goofy smiles!

With every step a brand new scheme,
We chase the dawn; it's like a dream.
In our jammies, we laugh and play,
What a cozy, magical day!

A Serene Stroll in Silky Threads

Silky ribbons, oh so bright,
We strut around, what a sight!
In our nightwear, confidence soars,
Hopping through imaginary doors.

Slippers squeak on cozy floors,
A mishap here, oh, who knows more?
A tumble here, a giggle there,
In our wardrobe quite the share!

Starlit skies, we dance about,
Then a snack, with a gleeful shout.
With cookies crumbled in our lap,
We're ultimate champions of the nap!

Through the living room we glide,
In silky threads, we feel the pride.
A frolic and tumble, what's your bid?
Join the fun, oh, just admit!

Adventures of the Sleepy Traveler

Embarking on travels in fuzzy gear,
With breakfast brews and yawned cheer.
Our ticket's stamped in chocolate chips,
Adventures start from lazy slips!

Stopping for snacks at every bend,
With sleepy eyes, but joy to send.
In every corner, magic looms,
As we tumble through our cozy rooms!

So many places to stretch and crawl,
In our pajamas, we conquer all.
With whispers shared and secrets kept,
A map of dreams where laughter's leapt!

The sun sets low, curtains drawn wide,
In pajamas, we sip tea with pride.
Adventures pause, just as they started,
In our sleepy realm, we are the hearted!

Dreams in Nightwear

In soft cotton, we drift and sway,
Through dreamy realms where we play.
Pajama-clad, we roam the skies,
A world of laughter where fun defies!

Bouncing on clouds of marshmallow fluff,
With sleepy giggles, we can't get enough.
Whispers of dreams, soft and light,
We twirl in the colors of the night.

Chasing rainbows, silly and bright,
In our nightwear, we take flight.
Together we'll spin 'round and 'round,
In this cozy, whimsical playground!

As dawn approaches, we'll cling tight,
But don't worry; we'll nap before light!
In dreams we find our silly flare,
In nightwear, life's beyond compare!

Dreamy Trails in Fuzzy Slippers

In fuzzy slippers, we take flight,
With dreams that sparkle, oh so bright.
We glide through halls, avoiding chores,
In search of snacks and midnight doors.

The cat joins in, a plush brigade,
With sleepy faces, we parade.
The couch a mountain, oh what a thrill,
As we conquer kingdoms, quiet and still.

Pajama capes and pillow shields,
We're fearless knights on soft, warm fields.
With giggles echoing in the night,
We laugh at our cozy flight.

So here's to trails of cotton delight,
To dreams and snacks in the pale moonlight.
In fuzzy slippers, freedom's found,
A world of laughter, spun around.

Midnight Adventures in Cozy Threads

In threads so cozy, we prepare,
For midnight quests, let's get out there!
With cereal bins as treasure chests,
We plot our course for midnight quests.

The fridge a portal to delights,
In our soft gear, we steal the nights.
We dance with shadows, twirl with glee,
In our pajama realms, wild and free.

Every creak of floorboards feels like fate,
As we engage, our giggles infiltrate.
The living room becomes a grand stage,
As we script our tales on the pajama page.

So grab your slippers, let's not delay,
In cozy threads, we'll find our way.
With laughter bubbling, let's ignite this blend,
Of midnight magic that will never end.

The Quest of the Comfy Wanderer

A comfy wanderer set to roam,
In flannel clouds, I find my home.
With socks as shields and hoodies tight,
I travel realms through soft twilight.

The hallway stretches like a mile,
Every door a chance to smile.
The world outside can wait and see,
In my pajama realm, I'm truly free.

Adventures bloom in sleepy sights,
As I brave the chill of midnight nights.
With a kid's heart and adult's dream,
I seek the thrill of marshmallow cream.

So join the quest, oh sleepy friends,
In comfy threads, the fun transcends.
For every corner holds a cheer,
In our wanderer's world, we persevere.

Slumbering Roads and Starry Skies

On slumbering roads where dreams collide,
In pajama valleys, we take pride.
With starry skies our blanket spread,
We frolic freely, no tears to shed.

In sleepy towns, we sip warm tea,
Crafting stories for you and me.
Each pillow fort, a fortress grand,
Where whimsical fancies hand in hand.

The moon a guide to every quest,
In cozy clothes, we find our best.
With teddy bears as trusty steeds,
We ride the waves of nighttime leads.

So let's embark on this jovial ride,
In slumbering roads where fun won't hide.
With laughter ringing, hearts so spry,
Under stars and clouds, we'll fly high.

Layers of Imagination

In cozy threads, we roam the halls,
With sleepy grins and cotton balls.
A treasure map on a sofa bright,
We sail the seas of a pillow fight.

Worn outside, they cause a grin,
Adventures start where dreams begin.
With every twist, a giggle shared,
In soft attire, we're never scared.

Through cereal ports and juicebox streams,
Riding wild on waffle dreams.
The world unfolds in snuggly styles,
In pajamas, we conquer miles.

Each day a quest in fuzzy gear,
With every step, our fears disappear.
So who needs shoes in this great affair?
With hearts so light, we float on air!

Daring in the Dusk

Under stars, wearing polka dots,
We chase the moon, forget our spots.
A sneaky cat with a feathered tail,
  In jammies bright, we set the sail.

With secret maps drawn on the floor,
A leap of faith, we dare explore.
In the garden hide, beneath the tree,
  Wearing capes made of soft T.V.

The shadows dance, a playful sight,
As we embrace the coming night.
With every step, the laughter grows,
  In wobbly steps, a daring prose.

So shush your dreams, we're on our way,
In jammies, we'll dance till the break of day.
With each heartbeat, a vibrant rush,
  In this jolly game, we joyfully hush!

The Silk-Sown Journey

In silky threads, the world awaits,
With fuzzy socks and happy states.
Each journey starts with a playful tease,
In pajama swag, we do as we please.

A dragon's land in our own backyard,
With each slide down, we play our card.
Cups of cocoa and giggly cheer,
In comfort, bold, we banish fear.

The silk sows laughter, the seams of delight,
In shades of neon, we shine so bright.
Through living rooms and kitchen fests,
Pajamas rule, we pass the tests.

So let's jump high in our feather-light suits,
With every twist, we raise our flutes.
On this ride of whimsy, we'll never tire,
In our jammies warm, we dare to inspire!

Fleecy Footsteps Across Time

In fleecy warmth, our spirits sway,
We wander paths of yesterday.
In ancient lands of bedtime tales,
Where every sock is full of gales.

With buttons bright and prints so bold,
We're brave explorers, watch us unfold.
Each step we take, a story's spun,
In fluff and fun, we've already won.

Through time we travel, unafraid,
With open hearts and plans well-laid.
Around the couch, we make a turn,
In softest fibers, our hopes now burn.

So raise a cheer with every stride,
In comfy gear, we take the ride.
Our journey's sweet, our laughter chimes,
Fleecy footsteps dance through times!

The Pajama Trailblazer

In cozy threads, I stride with flair,
Adventures call from my bedroom chair.
With slippers on, I lead the pack,
No day is dull when comfort's intact.

Socks that clash, but who cares now?
I'm the king of lazy, take a bow.
My blanket cape flutters in the breeze,
Saving the world with such great ease!

Each cereal run, a daunting feat,
Navigating through sticky kitchen heat.
With cereal courage, I seize the day,
In jammies, joy finds its own way.

So if you wonder, what's next in store?
Join the pajama quest—there's always more!
With laughter, snacks, and pajama cheer,
The trailblazer's path is ever clear!

Daydreams in the Dark

Under stars in my cozy nest,
I sit and dream, it's for the best.
Pillows piled high, a soft fortress wide,
Adventure awaits on the sleep-time tide.

Aliens dance in night's gentle glow,
In fuzzy pants, I steal the show.
With popcorn clouds and soda seas,
Anything's possible, so let it be!

A dragon roams the vast, soft land,
With gummy bears as my brave command.
Together we soar through snoozing skies,
Pajama world, where laughter lies.

When morning breaks, I'll still be there,
In dreamy lands, without a care.
For every sleep is another delight,
In sleepy realms, daydreams take flight!

The Comforter's Voyage

Set sail on the sea of soft and snug,
Where pillows drift like a perfect hug.
The sheets are my sails, the bed my boat,
In the waves of comfort, I gently float.

I navigate snacks on my travels of fun,
Finding lost remotes is never done.
A treasure map drawn on my cozy quilt,
Leading to mysteries with every tilt.

With teddy bears as my loyal crew,
Exploring the land of what snacks can do.
Each munch and crunch is a victory sweet,
A quest for the snacks that I always greet.

As night whispers softly, I drop anchor tight,
The comforter's voyage ends with goodnight.
In jammies, I sail the dreamers' sea,
Where laughter and joy are forever free!

Footprints in Fleece

In fleece-lined paths, I boldly roam,
Exploring the wilds of my happy home.
With each little step, I leave my mark,
Wandering through dreams, igniting a spark.

From couch to fridge, it's an epic quest,
Gathering snacks is truly the best.
With giggles and wiggles, I dance on my way,
In pajama prints, I make the day.

Every tiny footfall, a tale to tell,
In cozy attire, I know it well.
From the laundry basket to the TV stand,
Fleece footprints sparkle across the land.

So join my journey, don't miss the fun,
In fuzzy delights, the adventure has begun!
With laughter and warmth, let's giggle along,
In a world made of pajamas, we all belong!

Dreamscapes and Soft Soles

In fluffy dreams beneath the moon,
A dance of socks, a soft cocoon.
With every leap, I barely glide,
In pajamas, joy becomes my guide.

The fridge calls out, I heed the plea,
Slice of pie? Oh yes, for me!
With every step, I slip and slide,
In my soft soles, I take great pride.

The cat watches with amused disdain,
As I prance around, no hint of shame.
In the quest for milk, I rule the night,
In my cozy wear, I'm a silly sight.

So here I roam in my colorful spree,
While dreams and cookies dance with glee.
With each goofy stunt, I make a bet,
These soft soles will be my best duet.

Pajama Tales from the Twilight Trail

Under stars, I wander free,
In pajamas, just me and my tea.
A bear once laughed, a rabbit too,
I waved hello, oh, what a crew!

With every step, I accidentally trip,
Over bedtime toys, a wild whip.
They giggle softly, my clumsiness grand,
As I tumble down, they lend me a hand.

A squirrel shouts, 'Hey, what's your quest?'
I'm searching for snacks - I love a good fest!
In plaid and stripes, I surely confuse,
The critters cheer on my pajama ruse.

So here I roam, in whimsical cheer,
With friends of fur who draw near.
In twilight trails where laughter prevails,
The night is ours, oh, the stories it tales!

The Fuzzy Footed Odyssey

With fuzzy feet, I claim my throne,
A kingdom of couch, all my own.
Remote in hand, I start my quest,
To binge on shows, oh, what a fest!

The dog peeks up, quite confused,
As I leap over cushions, not diffused.
A snack I seek, a soda too,
In fuzzy footwear, I've no clue.

I conquer the fridge, a stealthy scene,
With stealthy snacking, I'm a king, a queen!
In pajamas adorned, I grab my treasure,
The sweetest bites bring boundless pleasure.

So join me now, in pajama style,
With laughter and snacks, let's stay a while.
For fuzzy adventures are the ones to keep,
In a world of dreams, where we all leap!

Starlit Steps in Cotton Clad

Under the stars in cotton I glide,
With laughter and whimsy, I take my stride.
Dancing shadows, a silly parade,
In the cozy fabric, my plans are made.

As moonlight flickers, I trip on the grass,
The neighbor chuckles, as I boldly pass.
A bear in pajamas? What a sight to behold,
With twinkling lights, the night unwinds bold.

I stumble across, a bubble of cheer,
The garden's a playground, so close, yet so near.
With every escapade, the laughter will grow,
In whimsical mischief, the night puts on a show.

So, come take my hand, let's frolic and play,
In cotton-clad magic, we'll dance till the day.
With starlit steps, there's joy to be found,
In our laughter and dreams, let's twirl all around!

Nocturnal Pilgrimage in Flannel

In cozy clothes, we roam the night,
With mismatched socks, a silly sight.
The moon our guide, no maps in hand,
Just snacks and laughs, across the land.

The stars above, they wink and tease,
While we groove under the gentle breeze.
Our pajamas glow, a fashion bold,
In dreams of adventures, stories unfold.

No worries here, just giggles fly,
As we chase fireflies in the sky.
A slumber party on the street,
With sleepy heads, it can't be beat.

Who knew that wander could feel so grand,
In pajama pants, we take a stand.
Each step a dance, a carefree spree,
In this flannel world, just you and me.

The Joy of Wandering in Woven Ease

With fluffy slippers on our feet,
We trot around, oh what a treat!
In woven ease, we prance and spin,
As laughter bubbles from within.

No tie or suit, just soft embrace,
In every corner, we leave a trace.
The world our playground, it's plain to see,
Adventures bloom in jammie glee.

The sun peeks out, we wave hello,
While clouds join in the fun, we know.
We'll chase our dreams with silly grins,
In comfy garb, where joy begins.

From backyard trails to kitchen flights,
Each moment shines, no end in sight.
With woven ease, let's laugh some more,
For happiness is worth exploring for.

Driftwood Days in Dreamy Wear

On sandy shores, we walk so slow,
In dreamy wear, where breezes blow.
With tousled hair and sandy toes,
We chase the waves, as laughter flows.

The sun sets low, a painted sky,
We gather driftwood, oh my, oh my!
In pajama shorts or fuzzy tees,
Creating tales with ocean breeze.

Seagulls squawk, they join our fun,
As we stack treasures, one by one.
No plan in mind, just glee and play,
Drifting through our pajama day.

With every splash, our spirits lift,
The sea's our muse, a precious gift.
In dreamy wear, we let it flow,
With driftwood dreams, our hearts aglow.

The Laid-back Explorer's Handbook

Step right up, here's the guide,
To lazy quests, where joy resides.
In fabulous jammies, you'll find your strength,
Exploring life at a cozy length.

The map is drawn with crayon flair,
To snack-filled trails, we journey fair.
With capes of blankets, we soar so high,
In our laid-back crew, we touch the sky.

From couch to fridge, adventures bloom,
No need for compass—just follow the boom!
With giggles bright, we sail the day,
In this explorer's handbook, we find our way.

So raise your mug of cocoa cheer,
In our happy haven, we'll persevere.
With every sniff of freshly baked bread,
Laid-back explorers, in dreams we tread.

Twilight Travels in Thread

In the glow of stars, I roam,
Pajamas soft, my nighttime home.
With slippers on, I skip and sway,
Around the house, I prance and play.

Out to the fridge, my midnight quest,
For snacks and drinks, I'll do my best.
A yogurt cup, a cookie too,
In my cotton suit, I feel brand new.

The cat looks on, quite judgmental,
As I perform my dance, parental.
"Why not a jog?" she seems to say,
But I'm too comfy for that display.

So here I am, in cozy bliss,
In PJs, I can hardly miss.
With dreams to chase, I'll take my flight,
In dreams, I soar throughout the night.

Serenity Stitched Together

Stitched in comfort, I take sway,
Happiness found in threads today.
As I lounge with snacks in hand,
My pajamas reign, the softest brand.

Neighbors peek as I cut loose,
In polka dots or stripes, I choose.
They say I'm mad to dress like this,
But in my garb, there's purest bliss.

Midnight snacks and movie thrills,
A peaceful night that gently spills.
In cozy wear, my joys abound,
Laughter echoes all around.

While others toss and turn in bed,
I skip through dreams where angels tread.
With bright-eyed glee, I roam and dance,
In fluffy threads, I take my chance.

Therapies of the Night

The clock strikes twelve, it's therapy time,
In jammies soft, I feel sublime.
A blanket fort, my evening nest,
On pillows piled, I take my rest.

With ice cream tubs and a film or two,
I laugh aloud; it's just what I do.
No shame in being a night owl's friend,
In cozy garb, my worries mend.

I sip warm tea and giggle at jokes,
While said slippers make their squeaky pokes.
The world outside is fast asleep,
But here in PJs, fun runs deep.

With every stretch and every yawn,
I reinvent who I am at dawn.
In this whimsical, drowsy charm,
I find that laughter keeps me warm.

The Journey of the Drowsy Dreamer

I waddle through the evening air,
In flannel prints beyond compare.
With fuzzy socks, I roam the hall,
A sleepy dreamer, hear my call.

From bed to snack, it's quite the trek,
I'd rather nap, but what the heck?
A midnight rant with cereals bold,
In my pajamas, stories unfold.

TV on, my trusty guide,
In this cocoon, I take my ride.
While others snooze, I skip and weave,
In vibrant dreams, I laugh and believe.

So here's to nights, so soft and bright,
Where joy persists till morning's light.
In every giggle and sleepy cheer,
I dance through dreams, no need to veer.

Whimsical Wanderings in Pajamas

In soft cotton dreams I do roam,
With sleepy-eyed giggles, I call it home.
Each footstep a shuffle, each turn a surprise,
As my blanket cape flutters, I rise.

A sock on my foot, the other in hand,
I dance in the kitchen, I'm part of a band.
With cereal confetti and pajama parade,
I lead my odd troupe, it's fun to evade.

The cat thinks I'm crazy, the dog wants a bite,
As I prance in my jammies, what a sight!
The clock strikes a warning—"Oh no, not again!"
But I grin wide, let the shenanigans begin.

With stars in my hair and dreams in my pocket,
I'll sneak out the door, like a pajama rocket.
A realm of soft laughter and fluff to explore,
In this world of whimsy, I'm never a bore.

The Hidden Roads of Slumber

With furrowed brows and eyelids low,
I venture down paths where night breezes blow.
The toaster's a dragon, my slippers are mice,
Each corner conceals a new kind of spice.

The fridge whispers secrets, the cushions conspire,
My pajamas like armor, I dodge every choir.
In a battle of midnight snack and sweet dreams,
I giggle and tumble through whimsical schemes.

Pillows are castles, my bed is a throne,
I declare it a kingdom while snacking alone.
With a head full of wishes, and crumbs by my side,
In this sleepy old castle, I'm filled with pride.

Each journey I take, I bare it with cheer,
In the land of pajamas, there's nothing to fear.
The roads are all hidden, but my heart knows the way,
To the land of sweet slumber, where silliness stays.

Cozy Corners of the Universe

In a galaxy spun of flannel and thread,
I twirl with the planets from my cozy bed.
My spaceship's a pillow, my blanket a shield,
Defending my dreams as my worries yield.

Asteroids made of marshmallows zoom past,
I surf on the stars, oh what a blast!
With cookie comet dust and milk as my fuel,
In the cosmos of comfort, I'm nobody's fool.

The moon offers cookies; I nibble with glee,
As I float through the cosmos, just pajama-clad me.
Sing, laugh and frolic in zero-gravity fun,
Who knew that the universe shines in pajamas run?

So here in my corner, I happily dwell,
In the cozy nooks, under a magical spell.
With friends made of stardust, and laughter that's bright,
I'll journey forever through pajamas tonight.

Unraveled Adventures Await

In cozy apparel, I plot my next scheme,
With morning unfolding like a fantastical dream.
A leap from my bed, the backyard is wide,
Where mischief and giggles in sunlight collide.

With a trusty old cape made of grandma's quilt,
I'm off to explore where the butterflies wilt.
Each blade of grass whispers tales of delight,
As I gallivant boldly in the soft morning light.

I dodge every twig and leap over mud,
With socks on my feet, and my heart full of blood.
The squirrels throw acorns; I raise my small hand,
In this grand adventure, I take my own stand.

So fear not the mornings, dear pajama-clad kin,
For adventures await when you let fun begin.
In sneakers or slippers, with spirit to boot,
Life's magical journeys are always a hoot!

The Night's Tapestry of Travel

In the moonlight we roam,
In our jammies, snug as can be.
Slippers slide on tiled ground,
While we dream of travel, carefree.

Teddy bears serve as our guide,
Mapping out the couch to the chair.
Each snack stop is a grand feast,
Carpet islands, without a care.

With every step, giggles arise,
As we tumble into our beds.
Pajama capers full of fun,
Adventures vivid in our heads.

So here's to nights of silly schemes,
Where bedtime turns into playtime.
In our hearts, we're off to realms,
Wearing pajamas feels like prime!

Gossamer Travels

With twilight draped like a cape,
We float on clouds fluffy and soft.
Each step dances with stars,
In pajama dreams, we loft.

Through imaginary lands we sweep,
Where chocolate rivers always flow.
Stuffed pals at our side, we leap,
To places where giggle seeds grow.

Cereal mountains, sugar rush highs,
Pillow forts built in a flash.
Midnight snacks under the skies,
Time vanishes in this playful bash.

As night takes us on whimsical rides,
With laughter echoing in the air.
Our journey's wrapped in cozy pride,
Who needs clothes when pajamas are there?

Pajama Tales by Starlight

Wrapped in comfort, ready to fly,
With blankets piled high and tight.
We caper and chase the twinkling sky,
In a universe of sheer delight.

Pillow fights, a gentle war,
Who needs armor when we can shrug?
Instead of swords, we raise our snores,
Like knights in sheets, safe and snug.

Under starlit canopies, we drift,
Adventures whisper in the breeze.
As laughter lifts, it's the best gift,
In our fluffy realms, we'll tease.

So gather 'round for tales untold,
In pajamas, dreams take their flight.
Each bedtime story, bright and bold,
Our journey's woven through the night.

Sweaty Socks and Dreamy Footprints

Here we go, with socks askew,
As we run around the living room.
Each corner holds a treasure cue,
In this whirlwind of fun and gloom.

We leap across the floor like frogs,
With pirouettes that make us giggle.
Our feet, chaotic like a dogs,
In this performance, we could wriggle.

The carpets are launching pads we find,
For socked missions of epic gleam.
With slippers on some, and smiles so blind,
We dive headfirst into the dream.

Rambunctious steps leave trails so sweet,
Sweaty socks dancing with pride.
With every whirling moment complete,
Our pajama escapades won't subside.

Walks in Wonder

In cozy threads, we stroll the street,
With mismatched socks and slippers neat.
The world's a stage in soft attire,
Where giggles dance and spirits aspire.

Neighbors gawk; we wave with glee,
In pajamas bold, we roam so free!
Who needs shoes? We're on a quest,
To find the fun, and simply jest.

Each step we take, a silly spree,
Exploring life so joyfully.
Sliding down hills, what a sight,
In fluffy clothes, we own the night.

So join the crew, let's make a pact,
To wander far, in comfy act.
With laughter loud and spirits bright,
Our walks in wonder feel just right.

The Freedom of Fabric

Oh, what a world in stretch and seams,
Where freedom lives in cozy dreams.
A warm embrace, a wrap so fine,
In comfy wear, we boldly shine.

We twirl and leap in cotton bliss,
With every move, we can't resist.
Beneath the stars, we claim the night,
In our bold fabric, oh what a sight!

No ties or rules can hold us tight,
In robe and shorts, we take our flight.
Dancing on grass, we wedge a smile,
Embracing fun, we go each mile.

So raise a toast to our attire,
For in this garb, we roam the higher.
With laughter's ring and dreams that gleam,
We chase the joy, a pajama theme.

Whispered Paths of the Dreamer

On whispered paths, our giggles float,
In dreamy garb, we softly gloat.
With nightcaps worn and sleepy air,
Each step we take, no single care.

The moonlight glimmers on our way,
In cozy threads, we laugh and play.
Through fields of dreams, we wander wide,
In our soft wear, we dance with pride.

A chase with shadows, quick as thought,
In pajamas light, we seek our sought.
Every twinkle brings a scheme,
As we journey forth, it feels like dream.

So every whisper on the breeze,
Reminds us of our joyful tease.
In night's embrace, we find our song,
In this soft world, we truly belong.

Soft-Spoken Adventures

Adventure calls in soft embrace,
In pajamas bright, we find our place.
From kitchen quests to couch parades,
Our silly antics never fade.

We forge new trails in fuzzy shoes,
Through realms of snacks, we cannot lose.
With cereal capes and pillows high,
We scale the walls, just you and I.

The world transforms, a playground grand,
In our soft gear, together we stand.
With blankets held, we sail the seas,
Conquering couch with the greatest ease.

So let's embark on this soft spree,
In our funny garb, just you and me.
With laughter shared, and spirits free,
Each adventure's better in cozy spree.

Drifting Through Dreamscapes

In fuzzy socks I take my flight,
With stars and snacks as my delight.
Clouds are pillows, soft and round,
In slumber's realm, I'm heaven-bound.

I chase the moon on cotton beams,
Where laughter springs from silly dreams.
A dancing bear, a hat-wearing cat,
Join my pajama party, imagine that!

With marshmallow trees and candy streams,
I skip along with giggly screams.
In this kingdom, silk and fluff,
Every moment is just enough.

The waking world can wait outside,
For in my dreams, I take great pride.
With every stretch, I soar and glide,
In this adventure, I shall abide.

The Stitched Adventurer

In patterned pants, I roam with glee,
A hero stitched from thread and tea.
I ride on pillows, sail on sheets,
With every step, a laugh repeats.

A cape of flannel flaps in the breeze,
I take on dragons, if you please!
My trusty sidekick, a teddy bear,
We tackle quests without a care.

Through secret doors in my closet,
I find a world that's quite the comet.
With socks as shields and blankets wide,
We charge ahead with joyful pride.

Each creaky floor is a dragon's lair,
But in my jammies, I'm without a care.
Adventure calls at each dim light,
In soft attire, I own the night.

Wandering Through Wonderland

In my jammies, the whimsy starts,
With a tangerine cat and rushing carts.
We dance with rabbits, pirouette on grass,
In this curious place, time's sure to pass.

Tea cups twirl, and so do we,
With laughter that's as wild as the sea.
A hatter's hat, all floppy and bright,
Invites you to join this fun-filled night.

Through trails of cookies, we take a chance,
With each turn, it's a froggy dance.
As flamingos bend and hedgehogs roll,
In this land of dreams, we find our goal.

Unraveled fun beneath a sky so wide,
With each hop and skip, I feel the pride.
So here we bounce, with no need to fuss,
For in jammies, we explore and trust.

Under the Covers and Across the Lands

Beneath my quilt, a kingdom grows,
Where everything is silly, as everyone knows.
A throne of pillows, a scepter of snacks,
In my pajama realm, there are no lacks.

A grand expedition to the land of naps,
With unicorns and talking claps.
I ride on dreams, a marshmallow steed,
In quest of giggles, it's my heartfelt need.

Under the covers, I hold my court,
With laughter buzzing, a playful sort.
The world outside can wait in line,
For under these sheets, I feel just fine.

With whimsical tales and jesters bright,
We craft our magic in the night.
Adventure awaits, both near and far,
In my cozy world, I'm a shining star.

Comfort on the Move

In fluffy pants, I start my quest,
A cozy trip, I feel so blessed.
With mismatched socks and a sleepy grin,
Adventures await, let the fun begin!

The fridge is my first target today,
In search of snacks, I'll find my way.
An iced coffee drip, I charm with ease,
In my comfy gear, I feel the breeze.

Through living rooms and hallways wide,
I strut with pride, my newfound stride.
Neighbors peek out, they laugh and say,
'Look at that one, so bold and sway!'

Returning home, my mission's done,
In my pajamas, I've truly won.
With snacks in hand and laughter loud,
I sit back, comfy, feeling proud.

Pajama Perspectives

In the morning light, I stumble and trip,
A sight to behold in my pajamas' grip.
Slippers slide, I wobble and sway,
On this silly path, I laugh all day.

The dog looks up, he tilts his head,
'Is this a dance or a journey instead?'
With cereal bowls, I waddle and scoff,
'Just another day in this cozy cloth!'

Each corner I turn, I spy and glance,
With swing and sway, I take a chance.
Neighbors chuckle, "Is that a robe?"
I wink and giggle, "Yes, I'm in vogue!"

So join me now in this playful spree,
In pajamas bright, wild, and free.
Embrace the chuckles, let them unwind,
In the world of comfort, true joy we'll find!

The Wandering Sleepwalker

Awoken by breakfast's tempting call,
I stumble outside while I drop my shawl.
In sleepy bliss, I wander along,
An unplanned journey, a pajama song.

With bagels in hand, I strut through the park,
In the morning sun, I leave my mark.
A squirrel laughs as I pass on by,
'What a sight! Is she awake or fly?'

Friends wave hello with curious eyes,
In my beloved pjs, I'm the prize.
Who knew comfort could bring such cheer,
As onlookers chuckle, I hold back a tear.

So, cheers to the wanderers who roam in sleep,
The pajama adventurers, in laughter we leap.
For life's too short for only dressing right,
Let's all embrace the whimsical fright!

Swaying in Softness

Fluffy clouds on my legs, I sway,
My soft attire brightens the day.
With each jiggle, I giggle aloud,
Dancing through life, my heart feeling proud.

The world outside thinks I'm quite mad,
In polka dots and stripes, I'm never sad.
With coffee in hand and crumbs on my shirt,
Every misstep feels like playful mirth.

"Is she going out or staying in?"
My neighbors bet as I twirl and spin.
With a wink and a hold of the door,
I cruise to the mailbox, craving more.

Comfort is key in this vibrant style,
With laughter and joy, I go that extra mile.
So sway with me in your pajamas true,
In this whimsical journey, the fun's up to you!

The Twilight Trek

In fuzzy socks and shirts askew,
We venture forth in mismatched hue.
Every step a giggle, every turn a cheer,
Adventures await, there's nothing to fear.

With moonlight casting goofy shadows wide,
We leap over puddles, our fear set aside.
Laughing at squirrels who take us for nuts,
In our silly attire, we're all just...whatever cuts!

The stars our guide, the night our muse,
In wobbly dreams, we can't refuse.
Through corners of comfort, with cheerleading flair,
Every hop and skip lifts hearts in the air.

So here we roam in our nighttime clam,
Each quirky moment brings joy, oh, so grand.
When morning comes, we'll still be out,
In pajamas, my friend, we'll sing and we'll shout!

A Journey of Fabric and Fancy

With polka dots dancing and stripes so bold,
We strut in dreams and tales untold.
Adventures await on this soft, cozy ride,
In whimsical garb, we laugh with pride.

Through tangled streets of pillow fort fun,
Every step ricochets, is this really a run?
With mismatched shoes and a cape for flair,
We become heroes in midair, we swear!

Our journey's a quilt, patchworked in jest,
Every thread a giggle, a bright, happy quest.
From the fridge to the couch with a daring leap,
We conquer the snacks—no time for sleep!

Together we frolic, a joyous parade,
In fabric so fancy, our laughter won't fade.
With silly shenanigans on this soft thrill ride,
In comfy attire, with joy as our guide.

Lullabies on the Trail

In comfy threads, we wander wide,
Under stars, we strut with pride.
Sleepy towns and pillow fights,
With soft lullabies to greet the nights.

We sway like dreams in the midnight breeze,
With pajama-clad whispers and silly wheezes.
Each giggle echoes through the moonlit air,
Adventures fashionably funny, beyond compare!

Fluffy clouds roll above our heads,
While we tell tales in pajama threads.
Frosted snacks and warm hugs near,
Drifting off, but not without cheer!

Every step a dance, every laugh a song,
Wandering trails where we all belong.
Clad in our fineries, exploring the night,
With dreams lighting up the jovial flight.

Wrapped in Exploration

In robes like capes, we set the scene,
Exploring the backyard, feeling quite keen.
With night owls hooting and crickets that sing,
Together we find the joy that they bring.

Whisking past bushes and twinkly lights,
In our cozy attire, we reach new heights.
Jumping over puddles and skipping along,
Our spirits are high, our laughter is strong.

Through the garden of dreams, we chase the moon,
With every twist and turn, our hearts are in tune.
It's comfy and wild, a delightful mess,
Adventures wrapped up in this joyous dress.

So here's to the nights of whimsical fun,
In the fabric of friendship, our journey's begun.
With cushions for clouds and giggles to share,
In exploring our worlds, we find magic everywhere!

The Adventure of the Lounger's Footsteps

In my soft and fluffy gear,
I march without a care.
Through the living room, I steer,
Chasing crumbs with flair.

Pillow forts like castles rise,
Where dreams and snacks collide.
With each step, I disguise
A quest for sleep, my guide.

The mighty fridge my compass true,
A raid on yogurt, sweet and cold.
With pajama pride, I brew,
An expedition bold.

So here's to cozy wear that gleams,
Each step a wobbly dance.
Adventures crafted from sweet dreams,
In pajama-clad expanse.

Cozy Exploration Beneath the Covers

Beneath the sheets, my kingdom lies,
A treasure trove of fluff.
In every wrinkle, mystery flies,
The search for snacks is tough.

With pillows as my loyal crew,
We navigate the seam.
A tunnel formed, just us two,
With cocoa as our dream.

Sock puppets sing, they cheer me on,
As I stretch and sway.
In my fortress, the day is gone,
Fuzzy feet at play.

The scooch and wiggle, oh so grand,
I conquer every fold.
With snacks and smiles, I take my stand—
To boldly keep it cold!

Velvet Roads and Feathered Paths

On velvet roads of comfy fleece,
I glide without a sound.
Each step is soft, a gentle tease,
In wonderland, I'm bound.

The feathered paths lead far and wide,
To napping nooks of bliss.
Each cozy corner, I'll abide,
In dreams I cannot miss.

With every twist, the blanket glows,
A canopy of cheer.
The laughter spills, the joy just flows,
No need to disappear.

Joyful might of pajama knights,
With snacks and naps in tow.
In feathered bliss, we dance all night,
In warmth, together glow.

The Quest for the Perfect Blanket

In quiet quests, I hunt my prize,
A blanket soft and large.
The couch unfolds with sleepy sighs,
My lap is now in charge.

With crumpled maps and snack-filled swords,
I journey near and far.
Searching through fluff and cozy cords,
I consider a nap with flair.

Adventure calls from every seam,
Where blankets might conspire.
A fortress formed, a dreamer's theme,
To keep my heart on fire.

So here I lie, with crumbs in hand,
A quest forever clear.
In fabric realms, I make my stand—
The perfect blanket near!

Slippers on the Path

With slippers flapping, I take my stride,
Coffee cup in hand, I'm filled with pride.
The morning sun greets my cozy parade,
In pajamas snug, my worries do fade.

The cat gives a look, a judging stare,
While I prance outside without a care.
Neighbors peek out, their eyes wide with glee,
As I strut by like I'm on a marquee.

Birds start to chirp, they join in the fun,
While I dance in my jammies, just soaking in sun.
In this outfit of dreams, I've found my fame,
Who knew morning strolls could bring me such fame?

So here's to the morning, and livin' it slow,
In fuzzy attire, I'm reaping the dough.
With slippers on my feet, I'll savor each step,
In the world of the comfy, I'm truly adept.

The Cozy Odyssey

In my fluffy robe, I conquer the globe,
Wavy-haired adventurer, no need for a probe.
The fridge is my compass, snacks my delight,
As I venture through hallways, what a sight!

The toaster's a mountain, the couch is my ship,
With remote in hand, I take every trip.
Crewed by my dog, we sail seas of dreams,
Finding treasures in popcorn and chilly ice creams.

I leap over socks like a ninja in flight,
In the land of my living room, I reign through the night.
Socks on my feet and a grin on my face,
Who knew such a journey could feel like a race?

So here's to my travels, in comfort and cheer,
Navigating my casa with nothing to fear.
With giggles and snacks, I'm the queen of this quest,
In the realm of pajamas, I'm living my best!

Midnight Wanderlust

The clock strikes twelve, the adventure begins,
In pajamas I venture, where mischief wins.
The fridge is my destination, oh what a quest,
For snacks that are hidden, I'll give it my best.

A rogue chocolate bar, a leftover slice,
In the land of the kitchen, I'm feeling quite nice.
Under the moonlight, with crumbs on my chin,
This late-night escapade is where I begin.

My cat's my sidekick, he's prowling around,
In this midnight adventure, laughter's the sound.
We scour the cupboards, seeking delight,
In pajamas so warm, we're ready to bite.

So here's to the nights of whimsy and fun,
Where pajama-clad heroes outsmart everyone.
With snacks in our pockets and hearts full of cheer,
This midnight mischief we hold so dear!

Threads of Adventure

My jammies are woven with stitches of dreams,
Each thread tells a tale of laughter and schemes.
With a hood like a cape, I'm ready to fly,
Embarking on quests, my imagination high.

A quest to the sofa, that mountain so tall,
Where snacks greet me warmly, I'll conquer it all.
I leap over pillows, a hero in fluff,
In a world made of laughter, I can't get enough.

The clock starts to tick, the night wears a grin,
In cozy attire, let the fun times begin.
With a flashlight in hand, I seek hidden spots,
Exploring every nook, with giggles and thoughts.

So here's to the journeys in pajamas so bright,
Where laughter and joy take flight without fright.
With every soft thread, a story we weave,
In our cozy creations, we truly believe!

Threads That Bind and Wander

In fluffy threads we roam the night,
With mismatched socks, a comical sight.
Through the living room, we slide with glee,
In the realm of dreams, we're wild and free.

In every corner, an adventure awaits,
With a face mask on, we tempt our fates.
Jumping over pillows, dodging the cat,
In this pajama quest, we've all gone splat!

Snack breaks are crucial, we munch away,
In our cozy gear, we seize the day.
A quest for cookies, we waddle and creep,
Through fortresses built while others still sleep.

We may look absurd, but who really cares?
In our cotton cocoon, we float on air.
Hand in hand, we giggle and weave,
Together we conquer, make-believe!

Pajama Portals to the Unknown

With polka dots and stripes, we take a leap,
Into fairy tales that never sleep.
In a world of fluff, we slip and slide,
Through portals of dreams, our giggles collide.

A quest for treasure beneath the bed,
Where lost toys and socks come to dread.
Armed with a flashlight, we bravely explore,
In our cozy attire, we can't ask for more.

Clad in our best, we tell ghostly tales,
Of caped crusaders in odd-looking veils.
The dog is a dragon, the cat is a knight,
In this soft realm, everything's right!

As morning peeks in, we yawn and pretend,
This magical journey will never end.
With cheeks still aglow from our nighttime spree,
In the land of pajamas, we're always carefree!

The Feathered Trail

With feathers trailing as we dance about,
In nighttime's embrace, we giggle and shout.
Like sleepy birds in a frumpy flight,
Our pajamas flap, what a silly sight!

To the kitchen, we make our great escape,
In search of pancakes, dressed up in shape.
A sprinkle of chocolate, a dollop of cream,
In our dreamland garb, we reign supreme.

Slipping and sliding on the kitchen floor,
Each little giggle, we just want more.
With egg on our faces and laughter galore,
We bounce back to life, that's what we're here for!

As the sun starts to rise, our trail begins to fade,
With sleepy grins of the fun we've made.
In the echoing halls of our hearts so light,
We remember the fun and feel just right!

Comfort and Curiosity

In our fluffy jammies, we're brave little mice,
Curious creatures with a penchant for spice.
Exploring the corners of couch and floor,
For mysteries hiding behind the next door.

With cereal cups as our breakfast fuel,
Adventure awaits, oh, we're nobody's fool!
Each cupboard a portal to lands far away,
Where pancakes float softly and waffles play.

Teddy bears whisper secrets at night,
In our soft cocoon, everything feels right.
We whisper our dreams as we giggle aloud,
In pjs so silly, we stand out in a crowd.

As morning light peeks, we'll put on a show,
With routines in our jammies, our spirits aglow.
Together we laugh, discover, and cheer,
In this cozy adventure, we've nothing to fear!

Pajama Visions of Faraway Places

In soft cotton dreams, I take flight,
Wearing my pajamas, feeling just right.
A space explorer, I glide through the night,
With snack-filled pockets, oh, what a sight!

To Paris I wander, in fuzzy attire,
With croissants and coffee, my heart's on fire.
I wave to the Eiffel, my dreams never tire,
In slippers I dance, fueled by my desire.

On beaches of sand, I lounge with flair,
Building sandcastles, without any care.
In my striped pajamas, I'm free as the air,
Sipping on lemonade, sun-kissed everywhere.

From mountains to oceans, I boldly roam,
In my jammies, I've found my spirit's home.
With a goofy grin, I claim the whole dome,
Adventure's my purpose, no need for a tome.

Undercover Wanderlust

Sneaking past the cat, I tiptoe outside,
In matching pajamas, I slip and I glide.
Tonight's my big mission, so I cannot hide,
An undercover explorer on a thrilling ride!

The backyard becomes, a jungle so wide,
With sticks for my sword, I'm equipped with pride.
In my superhero jammies, I will not be denied,
Every shrub is a treasure, no need to abide.

To the land of cookie crumbs, I make my way,
A quest for the treats, oh what fun today!
With giggles and laughter, I leap and I sway,
In fuzzy pajama pants, I frolic and play.

But here comes the mom, with a frown and a stare,
"Time for bed!" she calls, as I dash with a flair.
Though my journeys may end, dreams soar in the air,
Adventure awaits, in pajamas we dare!

The Journey of the Restful Traveler

A traveler set forth with zest,
In a bright striped outfit, he looked his best.
With slippers that squeaked and a pillow in tow,
He strolled through the park, causing quite a show.

He ordered his coffee, in fuzzy attire,
The barista just laughed, saying, 'How sweet, a choir!'
He danced through the streets, his heart full of glee,
While folks stopped to giggle at the sight of he.

But little he knew, with that outfit on,
He'd become quite the meme, in a jammie dawn.
Each click of a camera, a flash in the night,
Gave him endless clout, oh what a delight!

So off they all went, in their towels and tees,
A parade of the comfy, a sight to please.
He waved them all on, as they joined in the fun,
In the wild world of pajamas, his day was won.

Pajama Dreams and Daylight Discoveries

In the still of the morn, with a yawn and a stretch,
He brewed up some joy, while his plans were sketched.
With polka-dot pants and a grin ear to ear,
He stepped out the door with nothing to fear.

Adventure awaited as the sun started bright,
In fuzzy slippers, he danced left and right.
Bouncing off curbs, he was ready to play,
Turning daily chores into games on the way.

From grocery aisles to the nearest café,
He borrowed the smiles of every passerby.
With each little misstep, a giggle or cheer,
He found joy in moments, from far and near.

His jammies were magic, a cloak made of bliss,
In the world of the mundane, he couldn't miss.
So off he strutted, a beacon of light,
In a land of somnolence, he danced through the night.

Comfort and Curiosity Under the Moon

Under the glow of the silvery night,
A fellow in pajamas took off in delight.
With a cape made of flannel and stars in his eyes,
He chased all his dreams beneath midnight skies.

He tiptoed through gardens with slippers so loud,
Startling the crickets, he felt like a crowd.
With each little venture, the world felt anew,
Even spotting a raccoon, who wore jammies too!

From the swing set to sandboxes, he flew,
A nighttime explorer, where few ever grew.
His laughter like starlight, brightening his path,
While the world chuckled softly, feeling his laugh.

So here's to the dreamers who wander the same,
In the jammies of comfort, they follow their flame.
Moonlit adventures, with hearts all aglow,
In the slumbering world, they harmlessly fro.

Nighttime Ventures in Jammies

When shadows grow long and the day takes a bow,
A pajama-clad hero pops out from a plow.
His mission was silly, but full of delight,
To conquer the twilight, by pillows held tight.

With a twirl and a leap, to the fridge he would dash,
His snacks were the treasures to make quite a splash.
In jammies so soft, he indulged in his feast,
While plotting grand quests, like a daring young beast.

The cat watched with envy, as he darted around,
Imagining journeys where no rules were found.
Each giggle a beacon, each snack a new prize,
In this whimsical world, where laughter defies.

When bedtime approached, he took one final run,
In the land of the pajamas, he'd had so much fun.
With dreams as his map, he drifted with glee,
In the warm embrace of the night's jubilee.

The Cotton Comfort Expedition

In soft attire, we embark with cheer,
Slippers on feet, there's nothing to fear.
The fridge is our guide, we wander and roam,
In search of snacks, we always feel home.

With every step, we wobble and sway,
While dodging obstacles that get in the way.
A cat on the couch, oh, what a surprise,
He joins our quest with his sleepy eyes.

From one room to another, it's quite a display,
As we slide 'cross the floor, in our fun-filled ballet.
With pillows as shields, we battle with grace,
In this grand adventure, we set our own pace.

So here's to our trips in pajamas so fine,
The journey is silly, but oh so divine.
We laugh at our antics, and joy fills the air,
In the land of the cozy, we know we're a pair.

Snuggly Sojourns Beyond

In our jammies, we travel, who needs to dress?
We drift 'round the house, creating a mess.
Cereal boxes, oh what a delight,
A culinary quest by the fridge's warm light.

Slipping and sliding, we race to the couch,
Each bump and each giggle makes us all slouch.
The dog gives a bark, he's part of our crew,
On this snuggly journey, we know what to do.

With chips in our pockets, and blankets galore,
We take on the world, but there's always room for more.
From kitchen to living room, we tag and we play,
In these cozy garments, we brighten the day.

So come join the fun, leave worries behind,
These sojourns of laughter are simply divine.
In pajamas we prance, we dance, and we smile,
For every small moment, we celebrate style.

Pajama-ed Paths of Discovery

With coffee in hand, we step out with flair,
In our jammies, we wander without any care.
Exploring the garden, we search for the bees,
In fluffy attire, we sway with the breeze.

The neighbors all chuckle, they grin and they gawk,
As we stroll around in our mismatched frocks.
A quest for adventure, our mission is clear,
To find the best spot for snacks and a beer.

We hike to the treehouse, oh what a sight,
Our fortress of pillows, a cozy delight.
With laughter aplenty and giggles combined,
In our comforting clothes, we feel so aligned.

So here's to the paths that we boldly pursue,
In pajamas that sparkle, in colors so true.
For every small trip, we conjure up fun,
In this world of adventure, we're never undone.

Veils of Sleepy Exploration

Wrapped in warm fabric, we start our expanse,
With sleepy eyes open, we dare to take a chance.
The couch is our ship on this ocean of dreams,
Where giggles and whispers float soft as moonbeams.

We voyage through hallways in fuzzy delight,
Trading stories of mischief on this starry night.
Empty ice cream bowls are our trophies today,
Each spoonful a victory, our own tasty display.

In search for the remote, we unearth the floor,
Under piles of laundry, oh what's in store?
Adventures await in our playful embrace,
As long as we're cozy, we're winning this race.

So here's to the trips in our playful gear,
Where laughter and joy spread holiday cheer.
With wild sleepy dreams and hearts feeling light,
We'll venture together, till morning's first light.

www.ingramcontent.com/pod-product-compliance
Lightning Source LLC
Chambersburg PA
CBHW051635160426
43209CB00004B/660